Whispers of Faith:
Poems for Little Hearts

Kailey Marshall

Copyright © Kailey Marshall 2025

All rights reserved. No part of this book may be reproduced or transmitted in any form or by any means without written permission from the author.

About the Author 2

Morning Affirmations: Who God Says I Am 3

Ready for the Day: Armor of God 9

A Heart for Jesus: The Gift of Salvation 15

Sleepy Time Thanks: A Child's Prayer 21

To all "my kids" I have taught over the years. May God bless you and keep you, and may you always remember the lessons we learned and the love God has for you.

About the Author

Kailey Marshall grew up in a small town outside of Dallas, TX, where she learned to have a strong work ethic from her parents and grew her imagination with her love of books. Working with children has been a passion for Kailey's entire life. She believes that children are precious gifts from God and has spent much of her adult life volunteering, teaching, and raising children.

Morning Affirmations: Who God Says I Am

Good morning, little blessing

Let's start the day today

With who God says we are

Loudly, we will say

God says I am worthy

He sent His son for me

God says I am loved

My heart jumps with glee

God says I am precious

He wants to guide my day

God says to follow Him

I am already on my way

God says I am wise

When I listen to His word

God says to be full of joy

I will speak and be heard

God says I am a blessing

He loved me from the start

God says I am pure

Because I follow His heart

As I leave my home this morning

And go about my day

I remember who God says I am

And I won't forget to pray

Ready for the Day: Armor of God

Getting ready for each day

I always start the same

I brush my teeth and comb my hair

And play a little game

When getting dressed each day

I like to play pretend

My clothes turn into Armor

In God, I can depend

My pants become the belt of truth

I wrap myself in knowledge

My shirt becomes the breastplate of righteousness

Which will never ever tarnish

My shoes are wrapped in the gospel of peace

I am ready to spread the news

My backpack transforms before my very eyes

A shield of faith ready to use

My hat makes a perfect helmet of salvation

As God protects my mind

But the Sword of the Spirit is my favorite

Because I can speak His word anytime

Now, I am dressed to face the day

The Armor of God prepares me

I cannot wait to tell my friends

My God will never fail me

A Heart for Jesus: The Gift of Salvation

For God so loved the world

He sent His only son

To die upon a cross so big

He saved us, everyone

He rose again to break the curse

That sat upon us all

Then sent down His Holy Spirit

As someone we can call

Jesus lives inside my heart

I talk to Him each day

He can come live inside you, too

All you have to do is pray

God forgive me of my sins

I want to live for You

I believe You sent Your son for me

It's Jesus I will choose

Sleepy Time Thanks: A Child's Prayer

Before I go to bed at night

I have some things to do

Brush my teeth and take a bath

Just to name a few

But after that, I climb into bed

And pray to God above

I thank Him for the things He gave

And remember all His love

Thank you, God, for loving me

For providing for each day

Thank you, God, for joy in my heart

No matter what others say

Thank you, God, for family

I know that I am loved

No matter what goes on each day

You are still the God above

Help me sleep and give me dreams

Of Heaven's shining gates

I trust my God to keep me safe

For He is never late